SILENT STRENGTH

Shadows of Domestic Violence and Workplace Bias

ELIA MENDOZA

Copyright © 2024 Elia Mendoza
All rights reserved
First Edition

Fulton Books
Meadville, PA

Published by Fulton Books 2024

ISBN 979-8-89221-569-5 (paperback)
ISBN 979-8-89221-980-8 (hardcover)
ISBN 979-8-89221-570-1 (digital)

Printed in the United States of America

CHAPTER 1

I must call someone, but how? I don't have a phone. As I open the door, the warmth of central California hits my face. It is dark and quiet as it always is in the middle of the orchards. Who could I ask for a phone? I never made any friends with the neighbors. I wasn't allowed; hell, I wasn't even allowed to take the garbage out.

As I walk next door, I ask myself, "How will I ask to use the phone? I don't even know her name." I think it was Elisa, Alissa. No, it was Elvira. What will she think of a woman in the twenty-first century without a phone?

With knots in my stomach, ashamed and broken, I muster up the courage to knock on the door. There is no movement inside. All the lights are off. I knock one more time, louder and harder. Tears roll down my cheeks. What if she doesn't open the door? What will I do? What if he comes back, and this time, he goes through with it? And if he does, what will happen to my children? Will he do the same to them?

My fear increases, the sound of my heartbeat gets louder, and before I know it, I'm banging on the door. I see lights inside, the door opens, and I can't speak. I see her worry on her face as she examines me from head to toe. My neck, arms, and wrists hurt; I must have bruises. Elvira reaches for my shoulder and pulls me in.

As I stand still in the leaving room, speechless, she puts a glass of water in my hand. It feels cold and comforting. I raise the glass and press it to my neck. It's relieving; the pain subsides for seconds. My comfort is interrupted by a distant voice, "Can I call someone for you?" I open my eyes and ask if I could make a call. With a gentle smile and pity in her eyes, Elvira hands me her phone. I dial my sister Amelia's number as she walks to sit on the couch. Amelia answers, and I break down. I don't have to explain. "Call the police," she says. I hang up. I turn to Elvira and ask to make another call. Elvira nods. I look down at the dial pad, and my heart raises. Thought after thought, what will happen to my children? How will I tell them about this when they are adults? Do I have to tell them? I take a deep breath and dial 911.

"Nine-one-one, what's your emergency?"

My voice trembles as I say, "My husband."

CHAPTER 2

I hand back the phone to Elvira.

"Thank you."

With worry in her voice, Elvira asks, "Did you get rid of anything he can use to hurt you?"

My mind goes back to that moment. "The police are on their way. They will take care of it. Thank you. I must go home to wait for them."

As I exit Elvira's home, I hear her voice, "Please let me know if you need anything at all."

I look back and thank her with a nod.

Walking back, I look down and notice I'm not wearing any shoes. I didn't notice before, but there are rocks and broken glass on the ground. I open the door to my house and run in to check on my children. They are both calm, sitting on their beds, hungry. They haven't had any milk all day, and since they are babies, they can barely eat solids. My heart aches, my children are hungry, and I don't have the means to go and buy them what they need. Blue-and-red lights sneak through the curtains, and a hard knock on the door follows. My heart nearly stops. I walk to the door and open it.

"Angelica Macias?"

"Yes."

"You made a domestic call."

As I try to articulate my words, I notice the officer's last name, Castillo, gave me a sense of peace, knowing he's familiar with the domestic violence part of the Latino culture.

"Yes, my husband tried to kill me."

"Are you hurt? Do you need to go to a hospital?"

"No, I'm not injured."

The officer relaxes a little and continues questioning the night events. "How did it all start? Please don't leave any details out."

Taking a deep breath and a sigh of relief, I start narrating that evening's events. "My husband didn't come home after work. He got home very late and was completely drunk."

"What's your husband's name?"

"Carlos Garibay," I reply with a sense of shame, lowering my head.

"Please continue," Officer Castillo says while writing on a spiral notepad.

With knots on my throat, I continue, "I saw he was drunk, and I asked if he had brought the milk for the kids. Out of nowhere, he grabs my arm and throws me to the wall. He starts yelling while punching the wall, 'Why don't you love me? When will you forget him?' I was scared for the kids in the other room. I kept wanting to get free from him to go with them, but the more I pushed him, the harder he'd pin me to the wall, puncturing my left arm with his nails.

SILENT STRENGTH

I screamed and pushed him off with all my might. As I rushed to the kids, he pulled me from my hair and threw me to the ground. He didn't come after me. Instead, he went to the bathroom and got in the shower. I started frantically looking for the car keys. I wasn't sure if I was going to just get the milk for the kids or if I was going to run away. The keys weren't anywhere. I slowly opened the bathroom door and saw the keys on top of the toilet next to the shower where he was. He saw me, and my heart jumped out of my chest. He couldn't get out of the shower, so he just took the keys to the shower with him. As I waited in the room with the kids to ask if I could go get milk for the kids, my arms started to burn. I looked at them, and they were bruised, and the left was bleeding. I touched the back of my head. It hurt. My hair hurt. I looked at my children, and at their young age, their eyes showed fear. My heart broke. The bathroom door opened. I jumped out and closed the kid's door as I left them in their room. I asked for the keys to go get the milk. He grabbed my right wrist and pulled me toward him. He mumbled in my face the words, 'You will never leave me.' I pulled away, but I was unable to free my wrist from his embrace. With his other hand, he reached to the kitchen counter and grabbed a vegetable knife. My heart was racing. I knew what was happening. As he brought the knife to my face and then to my chest, I could feel the cold steel penetrating my skin. The seconds seemed eternal. My mind raced with different thoughts of my children, growing up, alone, without a mother or a father. In the two years I've lived in this hell with this person, I've contemplated suicide many times and attempted it twice. But now, I'm afraid for my children. Will they be okay if this man takes my life? He had me pinned to the wall with a knife pointed at my chest. I couldn't speak. No words could come out of my mouth. As an act of God, my daughter yelled, 'Mom,' from the room. He retracted, grabbed the keys, and left. That's when I went to the neighbors to make the nine-one-one call."

As I look down at my bruised arms and bleeding shoulder, Officer Castillo says, "I'm going to take some photos of your bruised arms, wrists, hands, and neck." I put my hands around my neck. It burns. Vivid memories of his hands around my neck return. I exhale with tears in my eyes. As Officer Castillo takes photos of my bruises and the knife, I look over to see if my children are watching. I can't hear them. As soon as Officer Castillo completes the photos, I rush over to check on them. They aren't sleeping. They are seating in their own beds. Officer Castillo asks for the information of the car Carlos left on. I give him the car details and mention the car is under my father's name and I need it back. The officer asks me to step outside the house to complete a search for illegal drugs and other weapons Carlos could possibly have.

Waiting outside, leaning against a police car, one of the officers asks, "What do you plan on doing now?"

"First, I will move back to Washington, get a job, and go back to school."

The officer looks at me with a smile and says, "That's great. Don't be one of those single moms who after they escape a situation like this, they don't do anything with their lives and become part of the status."

I don't know what to say, but I know he is right; I am facing uncertainty, and I see a potential path in the future. The officer asks if I have any idea where my husband could be. The only person I could think of is his father. We haven't been in California long enough for him to make friendships.

"His father, Ramon, lives in a warehouse across from the prison on the way to town."

Officer Castillo takes note and asks, "Is there a number where we can contact you if we find him?"

I look down and say, "He doesn't let me have a phone or talk to anyone."

The officer looks up from his notepad and asks, "Can we call the number you dialed nine-one-one from?"

I nod in agreement and glance over to Elvira's house, wondering if she'll be okay with receiving a call from the police. As I look over, an officer is speaking with her and starts walking back to us.

The officer asks, "Did your husband threaten you against speaking to your neighbors?"

Nodding and with a broken voice, I say, "Yes."

Officer Castillo asks, "Can you tell us of one of the threats?"

I take a deep breath and recount, "A couple of weekends ago, the neighbors"—gesturing to the neighbors on the left—"had a party on the lawn right outside my bedroom. That Saturday afternoon, Carlos had planned to attend that party, as he was invited. We were getting ready to go, but he didn't like what I was wearing. He thought it was too provocative. He said I looked like a prostitute for not wearing any sleeves and for wearing small heels. Then he said only prostitutes wear lipstick or if there was someone at the party I wanted to impress. I rolled my eyes and tried to walk away, but he pulled me from the shirt and threw me against the window." I close my eyes, bringing back that memory. I can feel again the air sucked out of my lungs with the impact of my back against the window. I continue, "I quickly turned around, removed the curtains, and tried to scream for help, but I couldn't. He pulled me from my hair and covered my mouth with the other hand. The people outside saw it all."

Officer Castillo asked, "What else did he prevent you from?"

"I wasn't allowed to take the trash out or take the kids outside to the lawn during the day. He took the air out of the van tires so I wouldn't be able to drive it. I couldn't speak to the neighbors, and I couldn't do chores outside."

"Would you say your freedom was taken away from you?"

With a knot on my throat, I say, "Yes."

SILENT STRENGTH

A voice through the radio repeats some codes after saying my husband's name. Officer Castillo informs me, "We've found your car and your husband. We need you to identify him. We can give you a ride there, and you can pick up your car."

"Can I take my kids with me? I can't leave them alone."

"Unfortunately, our patrol cars are not built to carry children."

Exasperated, I look over to Elvira's home. There's still a light inside. "I'll take them to the neighbor," I said, hoping Elvira is willing to watch them.

I rush inside as the rest of the officers start to drive away. I put shoes and a sweater on my daughter and wrap my son, who doesn't walk yet with a blanket. I walk over to Elvira's house, carrying my son and holding my daughter's hand. Once again, I knock on Elvira's door. Elvira opens and invites me in.

I ask, "Can you please watch them? I need to go with the police."

"Yes, of course," Elvira says.

Hopeful, I ask, "Can you please give them warm milk?"

"Yes, I will," Elvira responds.

I thank her and walk out and get in the back seat of the patrol car.

CHAPTER 3

The back seat of the patrol car is hard and asphyxiating, and the siren lights are blinding. The way to town to the in-laws seems longer than usual. As we ride past endless crop fields, vivid memories of rides with Carlos and the kids come floating back, cutting my breath. In the middle of the endless fields, there's a robust almond tree, the same tree I stared at when I tried to jump out of the moving car. That tree represents life and happiness, a life I don't have. I was dead inside, trapped in a life I didn't want to continue. It was too painful to keep living. As I opened the car door, Carlos grabs my hair, pulling me back into the car.

The blue-and-red lights of the patrol car turn off, bringing me back to the present. I recognize this dirt side road. It's the entrance to Carlos's father. I look out the window. I see Officer Castillo speaking to Carlos in the patrol car. The car stops. The officer explains Carlos has been arrested, but I need to confirm they have the right person. I worry at the thought of having to be near him. I'm afraid, the same fear I felt when he had a knife to my chest. The officer looks at me and notices my fear.

"You don't have to get off the car." I look over and see Officer Castillo holding Carlos out of the patrol car. "Is that your husband?" the officer asks.

"Yes," I respond, knowing in my heart that will be the last time I'd see him.

It is a mix of relief and sadness for my children and what could have been. The officer nods at Officer Castillo, and he helps Carlos back into the car. The officer asks if that silver Chrysler is my vehicle. I say yes. I see Carlos's father get a container out of my car's trunk. The officer gets out and opens my door. I walk over with the officer to my car, turn it on, and realize the tank is empty. Taking a big breath and tipping my head back on the seat, I say, "It's empty." I'm so tired of failure after failure, now I don't know how to get back to my children. I put my hands on my face and start to sob. The officer steps back from the car and talks to Officer Castillo.

A few minutes later, Officer Castillo approaches my window and hands me $250. I take a breath of relief and ask where the money comes from.

"Your husband had it in his pocket, and since you are legally married, you're entitled to have it."

A rock has been lifted from my heart, and I say, "Thank you." I'm able to go get my children.

Once Carlos is taken away, I rush to the nearest gas station, pump gas, and buy milk. On the way back to get my children, my heart is broken but freed. My mind is flooded with a million thoughts;

I need to pack for the kids, for me. What do I take? What do we need? Should I go tonight? Or wait for tomorrow? I look around in the car. I should get rid of any illegal substance Carlos might have had left in here. When I open the glove box, the rattle noise of a bottle of pills stops all my racing thoughts. One memory comes back: a handful of pills in my right hand and a glass of water in the left. I can still taste the mouthful of pills, and suddenly, I find myself back in that deep, bottomless black hole. I shake my head and focus on getting to my children and making decisions. Everything is so dark. I glance at the clock in the dashboard; it's past midnight.

As I drive into the complex, the homes are dark, except Elvira's. There's a dim light in the living room. I pull into the driveway and walk over to Elvira's. I knock once, and Elvira opens the door. She doesn't say anything. She just signals to the couch where my children's were sleeping. I grab my daughter and take her back to the house. I open the door, and memories from earlier that night rush back. Taking a deep breath, I walk into the kids' room and lay my daughter on her bed. Walking back to the door, I stop for a second in front of the bathroom door. I can't help but wonder, *What if I hadn't tried to get the keys? Would he have gotten that mad to the point of wanting to kill me? Was it my fault?*

I keep walking out the door. Elvira's door is open. I walk in and pick up my son from the couch, wrapping his blanket over him.

"Thank you for everything."

Elvira replies, "Let me know if there's anything you need."

Walking back to the house, I ask myself, "What happens now?" I've been waiting for the opportunity to decide for myself the life I want for me and my children. But now, all I feel is pain, shame, and fear. My daughter is asleep in her bed. I walk in quietly and put my sleeping son in his. In my room, I just lay on the bed. I don't change into pajamas or wash my face. Although my life and my children's are in turmoil, as I lay in bed, I'm at peace. I'm not afraid he'll come to the room and assault me like he did for so long. Unconsciously, I fall asleep, alone, at peace.

CHAPTER 4

"Mama," I hear in the distance. "I need to wake up. Make food before he wakes up." Like lightning, I open my eyes with a gasp of air. He's gone. The memories from last night come floating in. "Mama," I hear again. I jump out of bed and rush to the kids' room. Their smiles when they first see me give me peace. It is all worth it, for them.

As I get the babies ready, I prepare myself mentally to face my husband's abusive father. Many thoughts of possible outcomes and his reaction cross my mind. We go into the kitchen to prepare breakfast. It's so peaceful. My children eat and I realize that I can freely eat whatever I want. I smile as the thought of taking a shower without being assaulted or harassed comes to my mind, just a relaxing shower. The kids watch TV, and I look forward to a shower alone.

The water caresses my body, and it feels like freedom. I close my eyes and let the water run through from head to toe without interruptions and without fear. The warm water stings the wounds on my shoulders but relaxes my bruised body. It has been the most relaxing shower in a long time. Amidst the comforting water embracing my body, the thought of having to see my still-husband's father makes me feel small. It is time to keep moving and confront whatever comes my way.

Driving to my kid's grandfather's is like driving back to a life I left last night and did not want to return to. The stories Carlos told me once of his father nearly killing his mother and all the abuse he and his siblings endured by his hand frightens me. I warn myself to not be there too long and not leave the car, and what else? Right, not turn off the car in case I need to make a run for it. And not let him take the kids out of the car. The pit in my stomach keeps getting deeper as we approach the driveway.

Pulling into the empty lot between two warehouses, he is standing there as if he is expecting me. I roll the window down and hand him the house key, letting him know I am leaving his son in jail. Ramon, my husband's father, very firmly and angrily asks, "How dare you stain my son's record by calling the cops on him?"

I had always respected Ramon, but this time, I have to respond, "Your son tried to kill me with a knife in front of the kids. He beats me since the beginning while pregnant, while pregnant and holding my daughter, for no reason at all. He would hit me, punch me, throw me against the wall, kick me, and now almost killed me. I couldn't care less about his record in this country."

Ramon tones down his voice as he says, "Well then, even if it's true that he tried to kill you, you work it out as a marriage." I couldn't help but shake my head in disbelief.

"Say goodbye to your grandchildren because I'm taking them."

He says his goodbye to the kids, and I drive out of there as fast as possible.

Back home, I feel a great sense of relief. I look around the house and start to think what we need to take and what is staying behind. Going through the kids' clothes, I expect nostalgia; but instead, I feel relief. I gather all the clothes and cook some corn for the road. I worry my kids won't sleep during the trip, a thirteen-hour trip. I'm loading the car, and neighbor Elvira comes out of her house. "I see you're leaving. I wish you the best." Two other neighbors I've only seen but haven't met approach me. "Oh, don't worry, he'll be back." I'm confused but keep doing my thing. The other woman, laughing, says, "Mine has been sent to jail many times but always comes back." I look up and pause. Shocked, I reply, "I won't be here when he comes back." The two women look at me surprised. They wish me a good trip and leave. Elvira smirks and walks back to her house.

Everything we need is loaded, just the essentials, nothing unnecessary. I have hope for the first time in a long time. I look toward the future, and somehow leaving this past is not as painful as I thought it would be. I just needed to be a little brave. The time to leave this town, this state, and this life arrives. The kids are sound asleep, and I calculate that we will be in the state of Washington in twelve hours.

CHAPTER 5

Driving into my small hometown, a feeling of uncertainty floods in making a pit in my stomach. As I travel down the streets, memories of a young love put a smile in my face. That smile is immediately erased by a painful memory. I do wonder what is of his life and hope he's happy. I start planning my day and my life: get a job, go back to school, and go to counseling to deal with the trauma. How will I do it all? I don't know if I'm strong enough. I must trust myself, trust that I can do anything I want. I keep pushing the thought of him out of my mind. I can't help but wonder how he's doing.

I arrive at my parent's home. They come out to greet me; and as they see the bruises on my arms, my neck, and my wrists, they hug me. My mom is strong. She will not shed a tear in front of anyone, but my dad is not. He cries while hugging me tightly. My sister Amelia arrives at the house and the same thing happens, but she is also strong and doesn't cry. She helps me settle into my old room. It is then that I realize I forgot to pack any of my underwear, no panties and no bras. My mom and sister start laughing, and I realize it's starting to feel like a new life, where there's laughter and happiness. I am content.

My hometown—a rural, agricultural, mostly Hispanic town—is very limited on work opportunities. Besides agriculture, fruit that is, the biggest employer is the school district. Opportunities are limited and mostly filled with recent high school graduates or through nepotism. I mean, this is a small town. Who would speak up? My parents have welcomed me and my children back home, but I cannot be a burden. I must provide for my children. I keep repeating to myself that this is temporary.

The job hunt begins. There are some openings for childcare assistance and support at the school district. It is summer break. These positions are for the next school year, in two months. I am discouraged but hopeful. I start the application process and send it in. The job descriptions for paraeducators and building secretaries state that without at least a two-year college degree, a competence test must be passed prior to a job offer. This is the first time I feel inferior in the workforce and realize that I need to pursue a higher education to provide for my children. Now I just wait for an interview or a response.

Living at my parents' home, I understand I need to pitch in with something. As what I hope will be a temporary solution, I apply for state assistance benefits, food stamps, Medicare, cash assistance, and childcare. Typically, small agricultural towns fall below the poverty line. My mother, Brenda, has a state-licensed child day-care home center. Her home was transformed into a business when my parents became US residents. Yes, I proudly am the daughter of two immigrants who came to this country looking for a better life.

Their story begins in 1980, an inspiring story that involved the birth of three girls in California and a son in Mexico after two deportations. Although I was born in California, after my father's second deportation, my parents (Brenda and David) decided to raise my two sisters (Amelia and Andrea), my brother (Victor), and I in the Sierra Mountains of Michoacan, Mexico. Later, when I was a toddler, my baby cousin (Antonio), who was only ten months old, joined our family and was raised by my parents like another son. Antonio is my little brother.

Growing up in nature, surrounded by clean, fresh air, trees, tropical fruits, and clear spring water rivers and lakes was like a piece of heaven. We had no electricity and no plumbing, but we kept in touch with the world through a battery-powered boom box. Our neighbors were at a walking distance of twenty minutes through the Sierra with rivers to cross, and they were family, aunts and uncles. Every now and then, we had family gatherings, where we ate our raised farm animals and our own grown vegetables. We weren't complete savages. There was a hostel with a distance of about two hours on horseback, where we stayed during the week for school and went back home for the weekends. We were poor, but we were the richest in nature, happiness, and love. After my tenth birthday, my parents brought us to the US in pursuit of a better education and better life.

The licensed home child day-care my mom established in her home was once racially profiled and discriminated against by the town's mayor, the WA State's Department of Social and Health Services, and ICE. Yes, ICE. All the licensed day-care centers were raided by the state and ICE at the same time, not only illegally by the state but also by ICE in accomplice with the town's mayor and local police. This was back in the early 2000s. The women whose rights were violated in such grotesque and illegal manner brought a suit against the state and, years later, won a settlement. My parents were able to pay off their home with this settlement.

Now back in this home with my children, I know I am fortunate.

CHAPTER 6

It is summertime, harvest season is about to start with cherries, then peaches and apples. I know I have no choice but to work in the orchards to feed my children. I haven't picked cherries or worked in the fields since high school with my parents. It is hard, painful physical labor. My sister Amelia, who also lives in this town in solidarity, goes to pick cherries with me. The summer climate in central WA is of extreme heat in the summer, with sunrises at 5:00 a.m. and sundowns at almost 10:00 p.m. State labor laws do not allow for outdoor labor directly on the sun past 100 degrees Fahrenheit; therefore, we woke up at 3:00 a.m. to pack a lunch and drive to the orchards. Picking cherries is difficult; it is a special skill. You must carry a nearly fifty-pound ladder and an up to sixty-pound bucket when full of cherries. Imagine climbing up and down the ladder at least five times around each cherry tree. Cherries cannot be damaged at all and must be pulled from the branch with the stem. In the summer, 95 degrees Fahrenheit are reached by ten or eleven in the morning.

Back then, there were no laws demanding a break or a lunch for workers when working on piece rate. My sister and I did not take breaks or lunch so we could pick as much fruit by the time it reached 100 degrees, which was typically by noon. After a couple of weeks, I receive my first paycheck, $340 for a week's worth of work. I am so disappointed. How can such difficult labor in a multibillion-dollar international industry pay the workers below a livable wage? Cherry harvest lasts about one month. I take a big breath, remind myself that this is temporary, and carry on.

The school district calls in early August to schedule an interview for the building secretary's position on the next day. I could not be more relieved and hopeful and so are my parents. The day of the interview arrives. I am a nervous wreck; I know I have the experience from my previous administrative position at a funeral home in Seattle, which I had to quit due to my husband's jealousy.

That morning when I quit, I was getting ready for work—normal office attire with a pair of heels and, why not, a little makeup. When he saw me, he was infuriated, pulled me from my right arm, and threw me against the fireplace's wall, my back hitting a shelf. The impact was so hard that I couldn't stand. I just fell to the ground. Carlos reached down and took the heels off my feet. While breaking the heel off one, he said, "Who do you want to look good for? Is he better than me?" I kept pleading to him to let me go to work. I didn't want to be late. His reaction was to kick me on the left inner thigh. The pain was so intense that I couldn't make a sound or move. I just felt cold and sweaty. It felt like I was looking down at my motionless body.

Sometime later, not sure how long, I felt my arms being pulled up. He was calling my name, telling me to go change, wash my face, and dress like a decent woman. I couldn't stand. After sitting for a few minutes just holding my thigh, I heard him rambling in my face. I couldn't make up anything he was saying. I wasn't in my body. He became angry at my silence, angry I wasn't crying. My body was in shock from the pain. There was no response. He held my face, puncturing my cheek with his nails, and yelled, "Wash off your face. You look like a puta." I blinked, trying to come to my senses, and he let go of me. With difficulty and with the most pain, I've felt since giving birth to my daughter, I got up and limped to the bathroom.

I got in the shower while still clothed but didn't realize it until it became difficult to move. I realized what had happened while my thigh was throbbing. I could barely move my leg. Removing wet clothes is difficult. After removing them, I scrubbed my face to remove all the makeup. Carlos barged in and abruptly opened the shower curtain, yelling, "Hurry up. I'm driving you to work."

After he walked out, I got out of the shower and wrapped myself in a towel. I limped my way to the bedroom. Staring at my closet, I tried to choose clothes that will be to his standards. My body cannot endure another beating and cannot be late to work. Putting on the pants carefully and trying not to look at the palm-sized red circle in my thigh, I closed my eyes; and with a deep breath, I pulled the pants up. As I tried to put on comfortable shoes, the pain intensified. I wondered, *How will I get through the workday?* Makeup and styled hair were now out of the question. I rubbed lotion on my face and arms and brushed back my wet long hair into a low ponytail.

I limped my way out of the room and grabbed my stuff to go. Carlos grabbed my daughter in the car seat. Naturally, I was in pain and limping. Carlos yelled, "Don't overexaggerate. It wasn't even that hard," referring to the kick. I held in my tears and pain.

On the way to work, he was silent, and I stared blankly out the window. Traffic slowed in an intersection, and a young white guy on the lane next to me noticed the tears in my eyes. His look changed to that of pity. He lowered his window and, in a loud whisper, said, "You're strong." Carlos noticed the driver was looking at me and asked in an accusatory voice, "Do you like him or what?" I didn't move. I ignored him.

Pulling into the parking lot of the funeral home, I told him to wait for me and that I will be back with something for him. With difficulty, I got off the car, limped into the office, and quit my job, without any notice.

My supervisor noticed my limp and my red and swollen eyes and asked, "Are you okay?"

With a trembling voice, I said, "Yes."

He realized I was nervous, and looking out the window, he noticed my husband was waiting. He said, "Save my number. Call me if you need help."

I said, "Thank you for everything," and left.

I got back in the car and told Carlos, "Let's go. I quit."

Carlos turned to me and asked, "Are you stupid? How are we paying rent?"

I looked at him and, fed-up, yelled, "If you don't want me to cry for help right now, let's go!"

Carlos turned on the car and drove.

CHAPTER 7

I pull out of the closet a professional outfit from my days working at the funeral home. It still fits. I don't have any high-heel shoes or any shoes other than the ones preapproved by Carlos. Looking at myself in the mirror, I realize I am still dressing like he wanted—"decent." I hate myself for it, but I did not shop for new clothes. Money has been tight.

With knots in my stomach, I ring the doorbell to the intermediate school. I am invited to the lobby in the office by the secretary. I recognize her. We went to school together from elementary through high school. We never talked, never got along. She was and still is beautiful and popular, while I was shy—an introvert. As I wait in the lobby to be called in for the interview, I rehearse in my head the common questions typically asked, *What are my strengths? My weaknesses?* And in between all that, I just pray I get the job. I need this job. I need to start earning my own way. The school principal steps out of his office and greets me with a firm handshake and eye contact. He seems like a nice person. "Thank you for coming. They say I'm the principal. I'm John," he smirks as he shows me into the conference room. The vice principal comes in after us and then the secretary. It seems like it takes hours, but they only ask five questions. The interview ends. The principal ushers me out the conference room and says he would call me within a week. I walk out the building, unsure of how the interview went. For now, the orchards until I find another job if this one doesn't call.

I do not hear back for the secretary position for a week; but one afternoon, the principal, John, calls and offers me the position. I accept immediately. And then I start in a week. A week! I have no office attire to wear to work. I guess I'll have to make with what I have until I get my first paycheck. I am overwhelmed with emotions. It finally feels like I can move on, like I can live on.

There is one person I wish I could share this news with—my high school sweetheart, Adam. Adam and I lived a short romance through high school. I was so in love. We got engaged, but it didn't work out. Although we hurt each other back then, there was always a kind of love wishing each other happiness and well-being. After returning to this town, I reach out to him to know how he is doing. I just need to know for some reason. He takes weeks to reply, but one day, he does. He has recently gone through a separation and is going through the hardest time of his life. All I could do is offer my support and be there for him. I know what he is going through and opt to not share this news with him. It feels great reconnecting with Adam. It just hurts that he is going through a painful situation like mine. We text and support each other, but neither one of us suggests seeing each other in person. I am afraid of my reaction when I finally see him after almost ten years. I am not sure if it is going to be rage, sadness, or love. I am curious to find out.

One day, after texting constantly for days, we decide to see each other. Neither one of us knows what to expect. We meet one early evening in a place called Las Antenas, a hill behind the high school in the orchards where people commonly go for exercise. We get there. We both get off our cars and hug each other for what felt like a short time. We hug tightly, not wanting to let go. His agitated breathing shows how much he is hurting from losing his girlfriend. It hurts to see him in this pain that I know all too well. We let go of the hug and kiss. This is a surprise, not at all what I expect, and I know not what he expects. That short kiss jump-starts old feelings I thought were long gone—the racing heart, stomach butterflies, and that feeling of an inexplicable happiness that rocked my heart. We then talk while holding each other. It just feels natural, as if the time hadn't passed for us, as if we are just picking up where we left off all those years ago but with all the pain and history we now carry. We say good night while hugging, and we both go back to our lives. That encounter feels like an anomaly in space, like something out of this world that could not happen again.

CHAPTER 8

The first day of work arrives. I am so nervous as I get ready. I walk into the building twenty minutes early and see the chaos in the school's office—letters and envelopes everywhere, stacks of files on top of the cabinets, unopened boxes on the floor, and support staff not knowing what to do. The school year for students is about to start. The second secretary, Olivia, trains me on the basic use of the students' database and pretty much tells me to "dig in" to the letters, address labeling, stuffing, and sealing. My experience as an administrator for the funeral home in Seattle is coming in handy. I know my way around office organization, computer systems, and project management. The support staff is amazing and starts to help. I feel productive again. I feel like I can do this job. I can succeed here.

The days go by, the office work is almost completed, and I have proven to know how to do my job and any task they throw at me, which is why budgets, finances, health records, and other tasks typically handled by many different staff makes it to my plate. I became efficient and known for showing results.

As a secretary, of course, some teachers make sure I know what my place is and that it is not that of an educated, paid more than a teacher. Some teachers, not all of them, are condescending, always make sure I know my grammar mistakes in all communication, make sure to repeat everything more than once so I would understand it, plain talk to my high school, Latina educational level, and always remind me that I am the secretary at their service.

One teacher in particular would come into the office in the mornings or during lunch when there are other district administrators or parents to berate us secretaries by making requests that of a personal assistant and humiliate us because we do not know the high-level vocabulary they used. Same with the district administrators, who mostly love looking down at secretaries and support staff.

One time, after certified mailings, I was called by the assistant superintendent, Tammy, to the district office. When I walked in, I was sent to the mail room. Tammy walked in looking frustrated and agitated. Tammy grabbed the stack of certified letters I had stuffed and labeled earlier that day.

Tammy pulled one out of the rubber banded stack and pointed to the green certified USPS mailing label and asked, "Do you know how to read?"

I looked up at her, and she was serious. She was waiting for an answer. I said in a confused tone, "Yes, I know how to read."

"Then why didn't you follow the instructions here"—pointing to the dotted line of the label—"where it says to fold on the dotted line?"

I tried to explain, "Well, it doesn't matter as long as the barcodes are showing on the front. I have always done it this way."

"I don't think so, 'missy.' Here's a blade. Please sit here. Peel each one of these labels on all these letters and replace them the correct way."

I could not believe what I was hearing. This was humiliating. I sat there, and as I tried to peel of one of them, I started to cry. I refused to do something I knew made no sense. I got up and walked across the hall to Secretary Norma. She saw my tears and asked me to sit. I told her what had just happened, and she was in disbelief. "Tammy is a bitch. Everyone here knows it, but I have never seen her humiliate anyone this way," Norma said in shock. I asked her to please call the local post office from her desk phone. The postal officer answered, and I asked if the letters will be returned if the labels were not folded on the dotted line. The postal officer responded, "No, as long as the barcode is visible in the front. It does not matter where the label is placed." I explained to Norma what the postal officer confirmed. I went to find Tammy to let her know I did not need to remove the labels. Her response was "Okay, I like good solutions." She turned away and walked back to her office. Tammy did not acknowledge the fact that I was crying or that she was wrong, no apology, no emotion at all.

I go back to the school and Principal John already knows of the situation; this district is great with gossip. John calls me into the office, apologizes for what I just went through, and assures me I won't go through something like that again.

I ask John, "Do you see how all support staff is treated by some of the teachers? We are sometimes treated as inferior coworkers. We are made fun of for our lack of grammar, pronunciation, and vocabulary. Sometimes our culture is also mocked, not only ours but also the students and the parents."

John looks down and says, "I think I know who you're talking about, and I will talk to them."

Days later, a training for teachers on sensitivity is scheduled. Olivia and I wonder what it's about. The vice principal, Edward, who is a kind person, explains it is a training on sensitivity and learning how to work together with people of all backgrounds, cultures, and education. Olivia and I look at each other surprised and worried this will bring some kind of retaliation from some of the teachers. The training lasts about an hour, and as teachers start to walk in, the hypocritical faces start to show. The specific "mean" teachers are now too nice. It is uncomfortable. As the days pass, the passive-aggressive attitudes turn the workplace hostile. Not only are the secretaries the administrators, nurses, parents, and teachers, but now we were also pacifiers.

CHAPTER 9

Work is turning to a hostile and unhealthy workplace. Support staff are blamed for mistakes in communication. We are dubbed the "princess" secretaries by other building secretaries and principals. We are talked down, looked down, and left out of important decisions. Olivia and I hold on as much as possible but enough is enough. We reach out the union representative and are advised to kindly and respectfully communicate our concerns. We do, with the help of John and Edward, but it is worse with the teachers and other building staff. Working together becomes a nightmare. Days get longer, and the months seem endless.

Getting home to my children after an exhausting day is my reminder and reasoning for staying at work. Work seems so easy in comparison to what my children and I have endured and what we would continue to endure in the future. I want something better. I want a better job, a bigger city, and better schools for my children. I know that for all of that to happen, I need to go back to school; otherwise, I would always be stuck in the same place and earning minimum wage. I want more.

For family and friends, working in the school makes them think it is already too good for someone like me, an abused single mother. That is the perception. I am a broken woman who needs all the help possible and is pitied. That pity keeps me from living and making friends. People are always curious and inquisitive. All family reunions are packed with questions, comments, and blame. To the older women in the family, they could not wrap their heads around me leaving the father of my children. I am judged and looked down as a poor single mom whose life is over, and all I could hope for is a man to rescue me from the shame. My own mother, whom I love, is still ashamed of me being a single mother. Catholicism teaches women to endure whatever hell their husbands put them through, and divorce or separation is considered a sin; therefore, it only brings shame to the family. Well, that is me. Yes, she understands I was nearly killed and knows it was the best for my children and myself, but now I am the sinner, the single mom who now has no future and can never hope for one.

Adam, he is a gift, always supporting me, always there to listen to me vent and to hug me whenever I need. We grow closer and closer. We are spending a lot of time together, going out and getting to know each other again after all those years. I know he is still in love with his ex-girlfriend, and I know I am just someone who is helping him through it; but for me, it is as if I never stopped loving him. I know that my ex-husband is only a rebound to get over Adam, and it does hurt loving him knowing he is in love with someone else. His obvious suffering is painful to watch. I want to erase it any way possible. I invest myself in giving him peace because my love isn't enough. We have a lot of fun. We go out on dates—watch movies, eat good food, and try new tequilas. While I am striving to heal him in the hopes he would see how I feel, he gives me back some of the self-esteem and confidence in myself. I feel beautiful again. I smile and laugh again. Adam is becoming an important part of my life, and I start to hope and imagine a life with him.

Things at work are getting worse by the day. One of the male teachers like to get too close to women, uncomfortably close, but the workplace hostility is the problem. The passive-aggressive attitude from some of the teachers, principals from other buildings, and administrators from the business office is draining. The hostility is affecting my work performance, my health, my mood, and the worst, the quality of my time dedicated to my children. While surrounded by all the negativity, I know in the experience I am gaining, I realize I am very good at managing the building's budget and finances; I see a career in finance or accounting. That night, I start shopping for online schools. Back then, these aren't very popular or credible but find one I see giving me a future.

CHAPTER 10

I am stuck, stuck in this town without opportunities and full of judgment, stuck in a job that treats me as an unintelligent and unreliable woman for being a single mom, stuck in a relationship without any kind of future, and stuck in an online school I can't keep up with due to work, home, and young kids. And finances, well, there's that too. My job is paying me just a little over minimum wage, enough to stay in the social services assistance programs but not nearly enough to support myself and my kids without them. I know it is time to move on and that means move away.

My sister Mirah hears I am looking for a move. She lives in a nearby city and thinks of a position opening soon at her workplace. Mirah is a line supervisor for one of the biggest fruit packing warehouses in the region. Mirah gets me an interview with her managers. I have no plan if I get the job. Where would I live? I can't afford an apartment, and living with my sister Mirah is not an option. She is also a single mom of three and lives in a one-bedroom small house. But the interview is the start.

The day of the interview arrives. As I drive to the city, more than obstacles, I see opportunities. No, I have no housing, no day care for my children, and no idea of what to do if I am hired. I arrive at the interview in the town of Naches. The product manager and the COO interview me for the position of production assistant and quality control secretary—two positions, paid for one. The product manager, Brett, and the COO, Breezy, are very nice and professional. I could see how much they appreciate my sister Mirah, and because of her, they are interviewing me. The position isn't open to other candidates. I am Latina, and I do have an accent. More so, when I'm angry or nervous and here, I am a nervous wreck. I could tell they are a little disappointed hearing my accent. Maybe they expect something else. The interview ends, and as always, they would call me. I drive back not knowing what to expect.

Two weeks later, I get a job offer, $3 more an hour than what I am making as a secretary. I accept the position. I ask for two weeks to appropriately give my two weeks' notice and help with the transition of training a new secretary.

I draft my resignation letter and hand it to Edward and John. They appreciate all my work during my two years of employment but understand I am capable and hungry for more. They understand this job and this town are holding me back from something greater. My position is posted, and the hiring and interviewing process start. My personal candidates whom I offer the position to are not interested. They see all the work and stress and rather not take on that job. As for day care and housing, my younger brother, Antonio, offers me a spare room in his two-bedroom apartment; and his mom, my aunt, would babysit my children.

The day to move arrives. The move is easy. We have no furniture. All our belongings still reduce to some full trash bags of clothes, shoes, and toiletries. But those trash bags are full of new possibilities—the possibility of a better education for my children, a better job with better income for me, more career options for me. I see a clearer future and am hopeful and excited for the first day at my new job.

CHAPTER 11

It is finally the first day at my new job. Yes, of course, I am nervous—new coworkers, new city, new life, new everything. But I am excited for a new challenge. As I arrive at the warehouse, Brett greets me and introduces me to the managers and the packing crews. My direct supervisor, Daniel, is a Latino and very young but seems very knowledgeable on all things apples. After introductions, I am shown to my workstation, a very small desk by the corner of the quality control lab and a very old and slow laptop. Unlike the public sector, the private sector is all about time is money, so I am given assignments to learn my way around the multiple software. I spend the rest of the day learning to navigate the apple-packing process from when the apples are loaded to a hauling truck in the orchard to when the packed apples are loaded to be distributed around the world. It is a complex process, and it is a huge responsibility, as it is practically a food processing plant. However, I am very disappointed to learn that there is no such thing as 100 percent organic apples.

In my small corner workstation on the window frame, my coworker, Andres, has a collection of multiple-colored rocks along with some apple and cherry samples. I couldn't help but stare at the rocks, the memory of my face burning and my ear ringing from that slap years ago freeze me for a few seconds.

My ex-husband, Carlos, and I collected some shaped rocks and shells during a walk on the beach in Seattle. At home, we wrote on them and painted some of them; they were a centerpiece decoration on the shelf on top of the fireplace in our apartment. On a Saturday morning, Carlos's boss came home to collect some painting materials Carlos was caring in the work van. Collen knocked; I opened the door. I had not met Collen before. I knew he did not speak Spanish, and Carlos barely spoke a few words in English, but somehow, they communicated and worked together. Collen's appearance was intimidating, very tall, red-haired Caucasian with a very deep voice. Carlos spoke highly of him and constantly mentioned how good a construction painter Collen was.

"I'm Collen, Carlos' boss. I'm here to pick up some of the painting equipment in the van."

"Carlos is in the shower. Would you like to come in and wait?"

Collen walked into the empty living room; we hadn't bought furniture yet. Collen in the living room with me alone made me anxious. I knew Carlos would get jealous and upset. I was afraid of his reaction.

"Carlos will be out shortly," I said while walking toward the room.

"Okay." Collen was surprised I was leaving him to wait alone in the living room.

Carlos came out of the shower in a towel.

"Your boss, Collen, is in the leaving room waiting for you. He wants some equipment from the van."

"Okay," Carlos said with a sigh of annoyance as he got dressed.

The sound of the rocks crashing to the ground broke the silence. Carlos and I looked at each other and shook our heads. Carlos rushed getting dressed and went out the living room to meet him. I couldn't hear them clearly, but after greeting each other, they walked out of the apartment. I then walked out the living room to see what had fallen. The rocks were back in their place, a little unorganized but unbroken. I heard footsteps approaching the front door. Anxious and afraid, I rushed back to the room.

Carlos walked into the room, looking and sounding pleased with the fact his boss came to our house to get the equipment. He felt trusted by his employer. Suddenly, his voice and face turned serious. His eyes turned narrow. His face got tense, his jaw clenched, and his complexion flushed. I immediately recognized this look; I knew what followed. With a racing heart, I thought to myself, *I didn't do anything. I was in the room the whole time. Why would he be angry?* He approached me and asked me with a clenched jaw, "Did you like him? Did you find him attractive?" I was shocked. I couldn't articulate any words. My silence only made him angrier. As he approached, I tried to retreat backward, but I was cornered between the vanity and the bed. He got closer and closer, and I couldn't speak or move. "Answer me!" as he yelled, he raised his right arm with an open hand and struck the left side of my face. My head jolted and my face stung. He mumbled something, but with the ringing in my left ear and the dizziness, I couldn't understand him. All I could do was hold my face and cry. "Why do you make me this mad? This is your fault!"

"Angelica," Daniel's voice pierces through the ringing in my ear, jolting me back to reality.

Fumbling, I answer, "Yes."

"Let's walk to the QC [quality control] lab, where you will be helping with testing on your spare time," Daniel instructs.

Within a few months, apple season is over, and all operations and all departments gear up for cherry season. The workers are excited. Everyone expresses this is the season when they get to work a lot of overtime and make good money in a month or less. I think of all the things I need to buy my kids: beds, clothes for the school year, and me, I could use some warm winter boots. I grow excited for the season as well. Cherry season kicks off. The new packing facility comes with new workstations and new duties.

Over the months, I have learned that people here are out for themselves. There is no teamwork, and management from all departments are out for each other, making the work for us support staff that much more difficult. The administrative office is practically nonexistent in the warehouse operations. They are condescending with all their requests and would take on every minuscule opportunity to show us, the support staff, how uneducated we are. Grower's accounting is especially good at letting us know we aren't accountants. My cherry duties included international inspection paperwork and records which cross over the grower's accounting and shipping departments; communication with them on a daily basis is necessary in this extremely fast environment. The accounting department is condescending, but the shipping office is bluntly rude. They would laugh in my face for any minor mistake on the paperwork.

Cherry season normally only lasts one and a half months, but it seems like it goes on for months. The condescending tone and mistreatment isn't enough. One time, the product manager, Brett, yes, that same one who hired me, made a racist comment toward Mexicans—a racist statement implying that because of my background, they could not expect more of me than what I was already giving. Marc, the Hispanic line supervisor, was present and stayed quite; everyone in the room stayed quiet. I walked out, crying, toward my car. I was sure I did not want to be part of that company anymore.

As I approached my car, I remembered I was all my kids had. I can't leave this job. How will I feed them if I did? I got in my car and cried for what felt like a long time. After that, I wiped my eyes, walked to the bathroom, and washed my face. I walked back to the cherry line as if nothing had happened. I started drafting an email to HR. I explained the condescending and mistreatment from the various department, the racist comments from a manager, and the silence from many other coworkers.

As a courtesy, prior to sending it to HR, I sent it to Brett. Brett called me to his office. Brett thanked me for bringing forward all my concerns but immediately started to make excuses for his racist comment by saying the usual, "I have a Hispanic girlfriend. I have Hispanic friends. I'm not racist, just unaware." After what seemed like a litany of excuses, he asked that before sending the email to HR, I remove the reference to racism. And I did. After all, he was the manager who hired me, and firing wasn't a problem for him.

Cherry season comes to an end, and operations continue with apple packing and so does my job search. Earlier that year, I had requested Brett to allow me to flex my schedule twice a week so I could attend tax evening classes; it was denied. As the administrator for the production department, I need to be present at the jobsite that one hour those two days.

The time for annual evaluations comes around, and I know that with that email to HR, my evaluation isn't going to score a lot of points. Daniel and Brett both are sure to tell me how excellent I am at my job and, of course, the things I could improve on. The most memorable is that I am too quiet around the men and that I wouldn't socialize or laugh at their jokes, misogynistic jokes I might add. I have no words. All I could say is "I'm an introvert. I can't help it." The job search once again begins. But this time, I am as determined as ever to have a career, not just a job; therefore, the search for an online school also begins.

CHAPTER 12

After a couple of job interviews in HR and administration in different industries, I start to lose hope. On a Tuesday morning, Karla, the HR director for the biggest apple packing company in the area, calls.

"Angelica, the CFO and I would like to invite you for an interview tomorrow afternoon if you're available."

Without hesitation, I say, "Yes."

After hanging up the phone, I call Daniel to ask him to meet me. Daniel comes into my corner desk area, and we take a walk to the cherry packing line.

"I'm looking for a job outside this organization."

"I saw that coming. Thank you for letting me know. I am looking for another job as well, but please don't tell anyone yet."

I can't say I am surprised; Daniel is good at his job, and there are no advancement opportunities here for anyone who isn't white.

"I'm happy for you. You can be so much more elsewhere. I have an interview tomorrow for a benefits specialist position in HR. I will leave part of the day."

"Okay, let Brett know you'll be out, and let him know when you comeback."

"I will. Thanks."

Daniel walks back to his office, and I go to lunch. "How will I tell Brett I will be out for a job interview? What if he fires me on the spot?" I am afraid to lose my job before getting another one.

But I have to face it, so I call Brett, "Brett, I have an appointment tomorrow. I need part of the day off."

"Okay, just let me or Daniel know when you're back."

That is it. He does not ask anything. I am relived.

The day of the interview arrives. I pray I would get the job. I need to move on. I need a better workplace. As I drive into the orchards, where the office is located, I review in my head the most commonly asked questions, "What is your biggest weakness? Why do you want to work in this organization?" My nerves increase by the minute. I pull into the parking lot of the rustic, cabin-wood office. I wait in the lobby, admiring the rustic and modern architecture. "Angelica, we are ready for you." A redheaded woman says and ushers me into a meeting room. Another typical interview, same questions, same answers, same order. I leave feeling discouraged. It does not seem like I am getting the position. I have no HR experience.

A week passes, and I have lost hope, and my job here is draining every light inside. One very cold morning, I fill in for the QCs, who couldn't make it to work due to weather inclement road conditions. During apple bin checks, I receive a call from Karla.

"Hello."

"Angelica? This is Karla. I'm calling because I would like to offer you the benefits specialist position. You will start with an hourly wage rate of $13.75 and a generous, no-cost health benefits packet, and you will be transitioned to a salaried employee within a year."

I think to myself, *Okay, it's only twenty-five cents over what I'm making here, but the no-cost health insurance is a good option for me since I haven't been feeling well lately, and I need to get out of this workplace. And becoming salaried after a year sounds great.* "I am happy to accept. I do need two weeks' notice at my current workplace."

"Yes, of course. We will set up your access accounts and your office space in the meantime."

I rush into my office and start drafting my resignation letter. I wish I could take one week off to rest and get ready for my next endeavors, but I cannot afford a week without pay. I print out my resignation letter and give it to Daniel. "I think this is the best option for you and me. I am also leaving in two weeks. We can do better." I am happy to hear Daniel is also moving on to a better workplace with more opportunities for growth.

The time comes to start my new job in human resources as the benefit specialist. Karol is very welcoming and so is everyone in the office. My first day is about learning the new mandatory Obamacare requirements. This company refuses until the last minute to offer health benefits to its employees. I mean, it is such a burden for a billionaire company. They opt for the catastrophic plan, which only saves the employer from the penalties, but it does absolutely nothing for the employee. My job is to get every employee—over two thousand across five different companies and three different control groups all over Central Washington—retroactively enrolled in the plan. Not only enroll but also calculate all their overdue fees. It is a challenge, but it is very clear the company only cares about the expense and not at all about doing the right thing by its employees making them richer by the minute.

After months of extremely hard work with the insurance company, outreach to employees, and recordkeeping, I catch up the company with enrollments avoiding thousands in penalties. The owners are ecstatic, my supervisor (Karol) is amazed, and the CFO is making plans to reroute the penalty funds. I am expecting at least a thank-you from the owners, but to my surprise, Karol takes the credit. The end-of-year bonus goes to her, and so does the recognition. After all, I am the assistant to Karol, without a degree, yet.

I lose hope in this company. I stop working overtime, and my productivity is reduced to only meeting expectations. This is noticed by supervisors, and I am moved out of the HR office to the shared area with the accountants. Here, I have other Latina coworkers

I could talk to, and we prefer our native language, Spanish. The non-Spanish speakers are offended they don't understand us and take it personally.

Karol calls me to her office one morning. "The girls downstairs expressed that they are offended and uncomfortable when you and Diana speak Spanish because they don't understand, and they feel as if you were talking about them."

"Are you serious? You're asking me to not speak in my native language, one of the reasons you hired me in the first place, to do outreach in Spanish to your Hispanic employees."

"Yes, and you should speak to them in Spanish when it is work related. But in the office, keep other's feelings in mind since they can't understand what you're saying."

"Yes, I will keep it in mind."

I walk out of the office trying to process all these feelings. I feel silenced, again, like I was with my ex-husband. Back at my desk, I go online to the EEOC; and yes, asking me to not speak my native language at work is a form of discrimination, and it is my right to file a complaint. I contemplate it, but if I do, I am going to be fired. To this company, everyone is replaceable. I suck it up, stay quiet, and only speak to close friends outside, during lunch and breaks. I work with headphones all day long.

The time for performance reviews comes. I am sure that although I am not getting recorded for my work, the company would at least make good on their hiring promise, making me a salaried employee

SILENT STRENGTH

with more benefits and bonuses. Karol calls me to the conference room and begins by thanking me for my hard work. "The owners agree that we will give you a raise of seventy-five cents on the hour with the opportunity to an end-of-year bonus." I roll my eyes, but it is pointless to say anything. It isn't going to change anything, and the culture here is that no employee goes directly to the owners. The supervisor is to block all of it. I leave the room disappointed, positive that I need to move on. Not only is my heritage not respected but I am also being taken advantage of.

During a lunch break, a coworker expresses his frustration with his review. The same thing happened to him: he was promised a lot but given very little. He is my subordinate. He would at times work for me. It is a shock when I learn he is making more per hour than I am. I know the wage gap between women and then Latinas exists, but this is discrimination. He is also looking for a new job.

CHAPTER 13

I keep searching and applying to different positions in the private sector and government. Nothing seems to work. I am growing increasingly frustrated at a workplace that doesn't value my work or me as an individual, with kids as a single mom, online school, and now with severe rheumatoid arthritis taking small doses of chemotherapy. It is too much. There are times I take walks through the orchards on my breaks to cry and release my emotions.

After many job applications and denials, an email from the state agency of labor safety comes in with an invitation for an interview. I immediately schedule the interview and request time off. Of course, I couldn't say it is for a job interview. The interview is very formal, with a panel of three state auditors. It is intimidating. Although I have the required accounting credits to perform audits, I have no auditing experience.

After the panel interview, there is an individual interview with the audit supervisor. This is much more casual, and I am able to ask more questions. Not to mention the supervisor is a Latina. I leave with a pretty good feeling about the interview and the job. I know it is something completely new, but I want to learn, plus there is no wage gap discrimination.

"I will contact your current employer and your references, and I will follow up with you in about a week."

"Thank you for your time. I look forward to your call."

This makes me nervous. Karol has a temper and is difficult to please and work with. She is completely unapproachable and is never on the employee's side. I am terrified of the retaliation or even the firing.

One morning, as I am walking to my desk and barely sitting down, Karol calls me, "Why is Alma from the labor department calling me, and why does she want a reference?" She is upset. I know it. I have ruined everyone's day in the office. She has that effect on the office's morale. People around me notice something isn't right.

"Can I come up to your office?"

"Ugh, yes." She is furious.

I walk in and explain, "I have applied to the labor department for an auditing position, I have goals I want to achieve, I just purchased my home, I am in school, and I want to work at a workplace where I will advance and reach other goals. You gave me this opportunity for which I am grateful, but this company did not make good on its hiring promise. Therefore, I will pursue what's best for me and my family."

"Well, you know we don't give out references, right?"

"Okay, you don't have to call Alma back. I will let her know you prefer not to take her call."

As I head out to the door, Karol says, "I'll call her back now."

"Thank you," I say and I leave her office.

Karol uses her speakerphone most of the time. I linger outside her office to see if I could hear her reference call. It's wrong, I know, but it is crucial for this position.

"Hi, this is Karol, Angelica's supervisor. I'm returning your call."

"Thank you for calling me back. Angelica applied for an auditing position, and I am doing reference checks."

"Well, she didn't even tell me she was looking for another job so that should tell you everything you need to know, and I don't have anything further to add. Have a good day."

Karol terminates the call without giving Alma a chance to speak. I think it is over and I will be fired. I continue trying to get through each day, avoiding any contact with Karol.

Two days later, Alma calls, "Angelica, I would like to offer you the position of auditor one in training with escalation to auditor three within a year."

"Yes!"

Alma smirks. Compensation and benefits are better than what I have at my current position, and it is an opportunity to grow my career. "I will see you in two weeks." I am so grateful and excited for this next challenge.

On the next day, I hand in my two-week's resignation notice. I peek into Karol's office.

"Do you have a minute to chat?"

"Yes, come in."

"I have accepted a position at the department of labor and safety. This is my resignation letter."

Karol reluctantly extends her hand to receive the resignation letter, her expression a mix of disappointment and frustration. As I hand her the paper, the air in this spacious office with a breathtaking view of the orchards seems to thicken with unresolved tension. She scans the contents of the letter, each word cutting through the professional facade. Karol's furrowed brow betrays the emotions beneath the surface. A sigh escapes her, and she meets my eyes, a silent exchange of unspoken words. The weight of the decision hangs in the air; and Karol, despite her discontent, manages a curt nod, signaling acknowledgment. In that moment, the office seems to hold its breath, witnessing the strained interaction between an employer and an employee parting ways.

"During these two weeks, I want you to write all your processes for all your duties, detailed processes because I will not have a replacement in less than two weeks for you to train."

"It's a lot of processes, Karol. I don't know if I will be able to complete them."

"I don't care. Write them all."

"Yes, I will. Excuse me."

I leave Karol's office with mixed emotions. I now have more work than I ever had. This week is administrative assistants recognition week. Every year, the company provides a celebratory lunch for all the support staff in the office. In the middle of the week, I am wondering why I haven't been invited to the event and why my lunch order isn't taken. I ask other coworkers and find out the only one excluded is me and another coworker who had also given her notice. This is retaliation. All that work, penalties averted, and employees helped mean nothing to this company.

This type of retaliation isn't enough. Management decides that I need to do some heavy-lifting work before parting ways. I am thrown into a boardroom, with thousands of envelopes to stuff and address. Not only that but I also answer countless calls in regard to the letters mailed and tracked. This is where I spend the lunch meant to thank and celebrate all the supporting staff.

I keep thinking to myself, *I should have just quit. All this retaliation could have been avoided.* That is my advice to my coworkers, "Quit. Don't give your notice. They will retaliate." And sure enough, months later, they quit, not resigned. As for Karol, outside work, she is a wonderful person, a very generous human who happens to be a woman trying to build her career in a male-dominated workforce. But still, I am counting the days and hours to leave this place.

CHAPTER 14

Nervous excitement pulses through me as I approach the government agency's building on my first day of work. This office is in downtown, in the not-so-glamorous area of downtown. This trashy front stands as a gateway to a new chapter in my career. My supervisor, Alma, is waiting for me at the employee-restricted access doors. She ushers me indoors and gives me a lanyard with my state employee ID and key. There are cubicles left and right, people working on their own, no conversations, pure silence apart from those on the phone with customers. My new colleagues greet me with a mix of curiosity and warmth, guiding me through the maze of cubicles to my assigned workspace. I am happy to see I am not the only Latina in the workplace. My next-cubicle neighbor, also an auditor, Juan, introduces himself in Spanish.

After endless forms and mandatory harassment, safety, and ethics training, the auditing training finally begins. The audits consist of accounting and policy reviews and the application of RCWs and WACs, and they all include site visits and in-person interviews. The negative perspective of an enforcing agency is getting to me. I could not have a public social life. There is constant harassment in social media and hostility with the audited firms. Many of the audit referrals come from investigators who act as private detectives out in the field.

One particular investigator's passive harassment takes the form of unwelcome looks, a gaze that seems to follow my every move, leaving me with a constant sense of unease. The discomfort deepens later on as he invades my personal space with an uncomfortably close proximity, oblivious to the boundaries that should define professional interactions. The office environment, once a space for collaboration and productivity, now feels tainted by his actions. The penetrating stares leave me with desire to go home and shower, and the invasive closeness when discussing cases erode my sense of confidence within the workplace. It's disheartening to witness the unspoken violation that mars what should be a neutral and respectful professional setting. My colleagues share uneasy glances, acknowledging the toxicity that has infiltrated our workspace. Within a few months, other female colleagues report the investigator's inappropriate behavior, and he is dismissed from his service post.

Two years into auditing work, COVID-19 claims the life of its first victim in Seattle. It is March, and per health directives, all at-risk populations are to be sent home. During this time, I am still taking a small dose of oral chemotherapy and immunosuppressants; therefore, I am sent home to continue with telework until further notice. All auditing work is suspended due to all the restrictions put in place in an effort to mitigate the health emergency. Naturally, I am bored watching training, after training, and some more training.

My supervisor, Alma, recommends I join a special task force, the emergency operations center, a task force created in response to the pandemic. This task force consists of managing volunteers from all other state agencies with the focus in health safety through enforcement with the goal of limiting exposure to the virus. The EOC operates with military-like precision, adapting strategies on the fly as the virus mutates and presents new challenges. Information flows like a lifeline, connecting decision-makers and responders in a real-time dance of shared insights. Amid the chaos, a sense of unity emerges. The shared purpose of saving lives transcends individual roles and titles. The high-paced task force becomes a symbol of resilience, showcasing the incredible capacity of humanity to come together in the face of crisis. As the battle wages on, our commitment remains unwavering. Lives are saved through the tireless efforts of those who refuse to relent in the face of adversity. In the end, it isn't just a response to a pandemic; it is a testament to the strength of the human spirit, exemplifying what can be achieved when a diverse group of individuals rallies around a common goal-saving lives. To this day, we are still a team and friends. We are still the EOC.

Naturally, responding to the pandemic helps me find my *ikigai*. I know that I want to continue to help the community and continue to make a positive impact within my Hispanic community. After the life-changing experience in the EOC and the leadership experience it gifted me, I am ready to go after a more rewarding career. I apply to an agency that specifically helps minority- and women-owned businesses. This is the next step for me, a place I would find empowering and rewarding.

Adam reappears in my life right before the pandemic—that's eight years after the last time I saw him. In the depths of my heart, I harbor a quiet and unconditional love for him, even as he finds solace in the warmth of someone else's affection. Our connection, obscured by the shadows of unspoken emotions, unfolds in the subtle nuances of our interactions. I observe from the sidelines, a silent ally in his pursuit of happiness. Each smile he shares with someone else is bittersweet, but I find solace in being an unwavering pillar of support. My love for him, though unreciprocated romantically, manifests itself through selfless gestures and genuine encouragement. My actions become a testament to the depth of my affection, a love that transcends the boundaries of romance. As he navigates his emotions with someone else, I am hopeful she is as in love with him as he is with her. Though my own heart may ache with unspoken desires, I take solace in the beauty of being an unconditional friend, providing support without expectations. In this one-sided love, I find strength in embracing the role of an unwavering companion, navigating the complexities of emotions with grace and understanding. Our journey, though marked

SILENT STRENGTH

by unrequited love on my part, is a testament to the enduring power of friendship and the resilience of a heart that continues to beat, steadfast in its support.

To this day, all I want is for Adam to be happy, with whomever and wherever.

CHAPTER 15

Now I have children, I am able to support myself, I have a job that is more than just a paycheck, and I have a friend whom I love unconditionally. Over the years, my journey as a single mom, the weight of judgment and criticism from old friends and family forms an unwelcome companion. The echoes of disapproval reverberate through conversations, painting me as an outsider in a world that once felt familiar. Those who once stood by me now cast shadows of judgment, their disapproving glances fueled by the choices I've made.

As a single mom, the societal expectations of conformity clash with the reality of my life, leaving me standing alone in the face of scrutiny. Family gatherings become a battleground of unspoken disapproval, their raised eyebrows and laded questions a constant reminder of their perceived shortcomings in my life. The absence of a partner and my departure from the Catholic faith draw disapproving whispers, creating an isolating sense of otherness. The once-vibrant circle of friends has dwindled, their absence leaving a void that is both tangible and isolating.

SILENT STRENGTH

The narrative of my life, as shaped by those around me, paints the picture of loneliness, as if my worth is diminished by the absence of a traditional family structure or a shared religious belief. During this isolation, however, I find strength in the love I pour into my role as a mother. The judgments may sting, but the resilience required for single parenthood fuels my determination to prove that my journey, though unconventional, is no less valid.

As I navigate this path alone, I discover the profound beauty of self-acceptance and the strength that comes from standing firm in my choices, despite the judgments that surround me. In the silence of societal disapproval, my identity as a single mom and my departure from tradition becomes a testament to my strength and unwavering authenticity. Now I can teach my daughter that no matter what tradition, family, or friends think of her, she will always be enough to be whoever she wants to be.

The end.

ABOUT THE AUTHOR

Elia Mendoza is a Latina, a tenacious single mother, and a survivor of domestic violence. Navigating the workplace and simultaneously pursuing online education and English being her second language have been a testament to her resilience. Despite facing biases that painted her as unintelligent and unreliable, she has triumphed over adversity. Through sharing her journey, she aims to break down stereotypes, uplift other Latinas, and inspire resilience in the face of workplace challenges.

Printed in the USA
CPSIA information can be obtained
at www.ICGtesting.com
CBHW031725241024
16327CB00024B/340